Babe and I

by Irene Vogel
illustrated by Craig Boldman

Decodable 27

McGraw Hill Education

Bothell, WA • Chicago, IL • Columbus, OH • New York, NY

MHEonline.com

McGraw-Hill Education

Send all inquiries to:
McGraw-Hill Education
8787 Orion Place
Columbus, OH 43240

ISBN: 978-0-02-138169-2
MHID: 0-02-138169-0

Printed in China

9 10 11 12 13 DSS 28 27 26 25 24

I am a big, big man.

I must be ten times the size of a big van.

A Pet Ox

I have a big pet ox named Babe.
What an ox!

Babe must be seven logs wide.
What can he do?

Babe Helps

He helps me cut the logs.
We can do jobs fast.

Babe can even make lakes!
He just steps on land.

We have lots of fun.

I am glad.